Life Errant

Life Errant

Poetry by: Cori June Thomas

Published by Cori Thomas

Cover art by Patrisha Quinton of Q Design Crew
Cover artist Website: www.qdesigncrew.com
Cover artist Social Media:
Instagram @ Q_Design_Crew
Facebook QDesignCrew

ISBN Paperback: 9798989367405
ISBN Ebook: 9798989367429

Author's Note:

Errant? Why such an old word? The title of this book hit me like it was delivered by the 2x4 of Inspiration. I've always loved to travel. I have, at times, felt completely at a loss about what to do in life and where my life was supposed to go, or like that one errant hair, a part of the group but never really fitting in with the rest. I have felt out of sorts and lost for far too long, or so frustrated with everything that I want to call out the bullshit of it all. There's a lot of bull out there (and some in here too probably).

I imagine that trying to find their way was kind of the point for knights to go errant: discover their purpose, who they wanted to be as a knight. (Or leave because they were too troublesome in court.) But I'm not a knight pledged to a lord or monarch. Therefore, I must find my adventure (or misadventure) in my own way. This poetry has taken a while to create, spanning decades; between 2000-2022. While they aren't in chronological order, they were my way of trying to find my place.

Dedicated to my Grandma and Nana

Nana, I wish I could have known you longer but am glad I got some of my talent from you, even if it wasn't 'your luck'.

Grandma, it's been a privilege to know you and like you wanted I'm putting my talent out there for the world to see not hording it all for myself, even if I am a book dragon.

Errant:

1.
a. behaving wrongly.
b. straying outside the proper path or bounds.
c. moving about aimlessly or irregularly.
d. Fallible

2.

traveling or given to traveling

--Merriam Webster Dictionary

Contents

Life Errant

There's a road,
Down which you shan't go.
Dread looms in the gray.

When do you start existing?
Gliding through life, never living.
Only surviving each day.

It starts you thinking:
"Life 'tis a journey,
I've lost my way."

Adventurer.
"Life Errant." Instead say.

Massive Aerodynamic Yowling

May

Hail, thunder roll, lightning strikes, wraparound rain
Winds in the jet stream circle, chasing tails.
Massive aerodynamic yowling
for the Midwest.
May for the alley,
who knows too much.
The storms, destruction.
We clean it up.
Together, apart
Never alone
Such
as
it
is
The season of tornadoes lasts nine months.

Deep Sea

Deep is the sea
Witness the tides.
Wishing an impossibility.
A fin I want, no legs for me
Forever, I am; to live 'neath the sea.
In all my life,
Aimless, yes, true
Dreams of walking upon the land,
Youthful diversions lead—
O', how they haunt.
Hour upon hour, eternally,
Until time comes,
to trade legs and tails.
the water calling me.
While I wander and muse.
Impossible dreams
Of the sea deep blue.

Imposter Syndrome

The sun grays.
The moon rises.
All in all, there are no surprises.

Golden shades of molten days.
Silver lights of frigid nights.
Monsters obfuscate their blights.

The rhyming false
The rhythms forced
I am saddened with this farce.

Jumping parkour
badly hitting the rail
this poetry is
an epic fail.

Childish Games

Jump, clap your hands.
Find your partner and Do Si Do.
Roll away to a half sashay.
Hold together clasped wrists
Rover-red-rover
Can you send Joe John over?
Everyone and anyone
but no one at all
That is who will be at our ball.
Oodles of fun, none of the games
Don't worry all good,
Repeat and split,
In the end
It's all the same.

Time Moves Slowly

Time moves slowly,
Slow as a snail.
What makes it faster.
Is what makes it fail.
Concepts of time
constructs of space
so subjective.
What a disgrace.
Time warps,
slow, not fast-paced
Change my praxis,
change my fate.

Vines

In the city,
The streets are covered in vines.
Thick, dense
They strangle and mangle.
Choke.

The country plains are lakes,
deep as the sea
No footholds, no rest
Treading, struggling.
Drowning.

Farmland is oceans.
Cities are jungles
With misadventure comes
the hangman's noose,
or the riptide.

A Broken Compass

Arrow spinning
round 'n round
North, South, East, West
Nowhere to go
Everything, nothing to see
can't leave.
Don't make me,
Stay.
Go.

A broken compass
has no true north.
I'll travel,
By the sky.
I'm locked in,
maybe, hopefully
later, sooner?
Let's go.
Away.

Dearest One

My love, Dearest one
Together for all eternity,
walking along the heather.

Until we meet, heart in hand,
be true to me.
For I will be true to you.

Because it shall be sweet
Whenever we meet
To have love's first kiss with you.

Choices

The favored, the forsaken
Useful they'd be.
unless unwise—
Well, we'll see.

Kiss the majority of enemies.
Fight most friends.
Sometimes one is the other,
the change seamless 'til the end.

Sit in the room so lonesome.
Or act like never before,
ere all is forgotten,
like chalk on a wet floor.

Steal the luck of the lucky,
or make your own, your way.
left or right,
eventually
they're all the same.

Whichever path you take.
Whichever path you choose.
Revel in those choices
the ones, you make.

Tap, Tap, Tap

Tap, tap, tap
Tap, tap, click
Tap click click
The pen tapped a tattoo,
upon the desk
stuck not knowing,
what could, would, should happen next.

Tap tap,
Click, click, tap,
Click, tap, click,
The staccato of thinking
heard by all,
ignored by her.

Bored, Bored

Out of my mind
out of my skull.
The brink of
Sanity is such a scary place.
Bored
To distraction
unfortunately, nothing to distract,
me or others.
So bored!

How can I work?
I wait...
and...
...wait...

The clock ticks by
Tick.
Tock.
that damn clock
seconds
racing like a snail
chasing an abstraction.

World Goes By

As she sat waiting the world went by.
Too bad.

She never saw it,
sitting by the wayside.
Words undefined
she cannot tell anyone why,
she, voluntarily, sat sidelined.

That's not how it works.
Not how the story's supposed to go...
Nothing changes.

She sits watching the wall,
ignorant of the world outside the window.

What Am I Doing?

What am I doing?
The whys and what fors?
Dragging my heels
like an ass through stall doors.
What is wrong?
Physical, mental
I don't know.
Don't know.

What am I doing?
What was the plan?
Somehow it all fell through,
like sifting precious rocks from sand.
What to do with the pieces?
Let them lay.
pick 'em up.
I don't know
Don't know.

What *am* I doing?
Where do I go?
I'm lost.
Can't find my way.
What do I do?
I don't know.
I don't know.

Keeper of Secrets

Why does this happen to me?
All I do is sit, listen quietly.
They tell their stories, secrets, all to me.
Keeper of secrets is not who I want to be.

Once before I tried to talk to someone.
They did not wait or ask if I was done,
They interrupted, never listening.
Then told their dangerous secrets all to me.

I've been told too many things, you see.
Because, I'm told, no one holds my key
Although I no longer sit and listen quietly
Still, the secrets, they find a way to me.

Why, oh why, does this keep happening to me?
Keeper of the secrets is what they've made me.
All I can do is sit, listen silently dolefully.
Keeper of secrets is all I'll ever be.

Damn. What happened to others listening?

Betrayal

You unlocked my heart with a key,
and ripped it up in front of me.

I gave mostly everything you asked
I said no, you turned away,

"I hurt you,
make everything seem like a task."
I messed up
you made cruel jokes along the way.

When your boys came,
you dropped me like a sack.
Used as a stepping-stone,
on your life's track.

Lost

Lost, I'm lost.
I've lost my way.
Like a kite with no one to hold my string.
I'm lost in the wind.
No compass to point the way.
I don't know,
where to go.
Up and down
a spiral of emotion.
Nothing is ok.
Everything seems fine,
Except,
I've lost my way.
Like a boat in a storm
a tether cut.

Meandering

Plodding

Wondering

Aimless

Lost

Who am I?

Who am I?
Who, am I?
Is who I am decided by me?
Or is it determined by my friends, my family?
Is it a genetic thing?
DNA RNA, written out for all to see?
Is it how I was raised?
My loving family, and frenemies?
My interactions or lack thereof?
A chance to change or break free.
Half of one, a dozen of the other
Equal and not.
Do they both at the same time matter?
No matter, no mind.
It still does not
answer the question?
Who am I?

Seek

You seek the way,
yet cannot see
what is in front of you.
You look past,
without a second glance
don't fret others do it too.
Eyes skate away,
scanning middle ground.
What a weird way to quest.

Look to the past,
for a future bright
somehow nothing back there seems right.
And the hope that was promised
which was drilled into the head,
seems a pipe dream.
slipping between the fingers
Forever lost, in shifted sand.

BS Me

Bullshit me
All day long, at all times,
singing a grand ol' song,

Bullshit to me some more,
all over again,
unfazed at what might happen, caught once more.

Keep up with your bullshit.
Stretch that lie,
Gaslight, Blind me in the hazy fog.

Bullshit me 'til truth breaks.
As I watch and you—
Dig.
And dig.
A hole, deep, deep down
All the way past six under.

Proud American

To be a part of America
It makes me so proud to be in a nation, that
lets people believe, or disbelieve as they will, without
fear of persecution.
Except when it's beyond that which is comfortable to
so-called Christians.

So proud to be American.
Home of the free.
The freedom to think for oneself,
for those who think like chattel.

In a place like America.
So happy to be in the Great Melting Pot
where the individual is more important than
the group.
As long as they don't stray, too far from the ideal:
the mainstream.

The freedom of America.
How glad to be in a land, that fights for equality.
Unless it allows the minority to be as equal as
the majority.

So grateful to be American.
That my country helps its citizens most in need.
Once they helped their lobbyists who bought them
Leaving the rest picked over table scraps

Welcome one
Welcome the one percent.
Welcome to the New Age of America
Welcome
Welcome to the
Plutocratic Oligarchy of the
Divided States of America

As I Lay There Watching

As I lay there watching
Little did I know.
Real life I was witnessing.
Not a TV show.

As I lay there watching
Reality sinking in
What I took for fiction
Was not so sanguine.

As I lay there watching
Panic slowly setting in,
I prayed that my family
Would not wear cloaks of linen.

As I lay there watching
Two towers fell.
Paralyzed and helpless
I observed that fresh hell.

As I lay there watching
Horrors flood my mind,
Answers to a vivid nightmare
I thought I did find.

As I lay there watching
butt frozen to my chair
school seemed insignificant
nor be of any help or care.

As I lay there watching
My world crumbling down
Flashbacks I had to a building
That was bombed downtown.

As I again lay there watching
The world I know fall apart
Brick by brick I'd have to rebuild it

I checked out hard.

As I lay there watching
Cellphone in hand
Busy Busy
All lines flooded. *Bzzt....Bzzzt....*
Try, try again.
Bzzzt.....
B*zzzt*

Beware the Buyers

Beware those who buy and sell,
all that is around them.
For they put a price upon the soul.
Take care.
A soul is forever.
What happens to it,
is never forgotten.
Given time, with hard work,
It can be washed near anew.

Those that buy and sell know nothing...
They only want a soul.
Why?
To feed.
Feed their vanity, greed.
Lust. For power.
Keep thy soul, tis a treasure.
Or be the devoured.

Cold

The cold
Seeps into the bones
Sneaks into the home of the soul
Tries to eat the spirit.
Heat will dissipate, dissolve all in a puddle.
Cold compacts, devours,
Winds rend through,
Eating, biting flesh
Making you waste away,
Until all that's left is an empty, shivering shell.

Scattered

Scattered thoughts,
Scattered mind
Bees in a meadow
Drops of rain
Come back.
Collect.
Stay centered if not the same.

Scattered mind
Scattered thoughts
Changed by the wind
Tides. moon sways the sea.
Get back.
Steady.
Stay centered if not strange.

Scattered soul
Scattered brained
Open for all to see.
Wisps of marsh vapor
Pull back.
Grounded.
Stay centered, I plead.

A Lie

It is all a lie.
Why?
I do not know.
We lie all day,
at all times
to tell the truth,
should set you free.
Instead, you die.
Which, in a way, is freedom.
Fee of life.
Truth twisters and liars.

This is all a lie,
Facts are cherry-picked
fitting only the agenda pushed
gaslighting everything
and if you don't see it this way,
you're an idiot.
A fool.
A murderer.
A liar.

We are told all the lies.
That the world is black and white.
There are only two sides.
Ours.
Theirs.
And if you don't choose you are wrong.
Make sure what you pick
is the best choice.
There really is only one choice.
Mine.

The Liar.

A to B

Never easy to pick.
Do I want A or B?
Don't give a left or right.
I can pick or not,
my voice: A Choice.
one evil over another
to choose the next 'Anti-Christ'.
Who will lead?
Who's full of hot air?
Which to choose
who will be more, 'fair'?
I could say forget it,
for that is my right too.
Though feel a traitor—
rights abased.
Now I wonder if my say means anything.
I don't want a popularity contest.
Who will be more?
Who will work and strive for the all?
Someone not in the pocket of a lobbyist
Boughten, a good thrall.
Who to choose from this mass quantity?
To vote or not
that is my question.
which will carry the stick?
which will talk 'til face's blue?
Is there one that can do both,
know when it is time for the best tool?
if I chose, will they be the one?
Because I picked doesn't mean they've won.
The electoral college decides it anyway.
But, at least, my conscious is clear
I voted as is my right.
freedoms cost dear.
Whom will I vote for?
It is still not clear.
In knowledge, weighing each one.
Weighted their merit

judged their wrong
from my opinions and research
I will pick the one I want,
and try to respect the one who wins.
If all else fails, I will set my eyes on the
congress and senate.
Term limits without appeal.

See Me

Here I am
I'm waving and jumping.
Can you read?
The words are there.
An open book
Secretively open
Ready
No need for instruction.
Do you see the real me?
I am here.
You see.
You say you can,
I have doubts.
You try, right?
I don't lie.
I try not to.
Still no matter how hard I try.
You refuse to see
the real me.

Panic Attack

Why, why? Why does this fear rock me so?
Why does it send waves of panic and pain?
I want to curl up in a ball, rock away,
Fear is a bastard.
Panic a bitch.

Why do I fear?
What happened?
What can it be?
Was it ingrained in, or witnessed by me?
I don't know.
don't know.

This fear so irrational and real.
Will it happen?
Has it happened?
Would I remember if it did?
Panic, Panic,
Breathe Breathe
In and out, belly breaths
Long, deep, and slow breaths

Stop the shaking,
calm the crying,
It will be ok.
The fear will recede,
like the ocean's tide.
Underneath the surface
A tiger ready to pounce
Up the guard there it is
waiting and waiting
A stalker on the stairs

Panic! Panic!
Breathe, please, breathe

Calm down
Calm, cool, and collected,
Breathe in, Breathe out.

Muscles loosen,
please don't contract,
Don't tighten and shake
With this racking quaking
fear and panic

Panic! Panic!
Breathe! Damn it! Breathe!

Think forest and trees.
Think tranquil scenes.
Think of snow and burning fireplaces,
Think about serenity.

Stop this torture
Stop this sadness
Think instead of meadows in timbered mountains,
Think of woods and a hidden plain.
Waterfalls and quiet lakes,
with butterflies on flowers.
What beautiful things to see.

Remember just:
Breathe

Not Answers

The world is full of not-answers.
Which are almost worse than none
because they leave you with impressions
that you had one.
Until you think upon it
turning it in the mind.
Eventually you realize the substance
of the puff and fluff that was supplied.
There are those who are gifted
spinning silver out of rays of sun.
Giving lasting notions
they said something,
when their words were non—
And then there are the schemers,
with their boasts and praise
talking gaseous circles,
blaming you for misunderstanding
the confusions they proclaimed.

Thought Circles

RoundandRoundandRound

Warning and Advice

All she wanted was to warn.
Nothing more than that.
So, she used her own experience,
for she knew it to be true and fact.
Instead of taking and building on the advice she gave,
people rent and tore.
What else can be so hateful?
Then the closed minds, calling
every woman idiot and whore?
Just because you don't acknowledge,
does not mean the danger is less real.
Even if it is not supposed to
it can happen here still.
Not everyone wants the limelight
ShOcKiNg, yes, I know.
There is nothing wrong with awareness,
it may save a life.
I would want that for my son and friend's wife.
Roads are meant for travel
criminals take them too.
Why surprised that America's crossroads
are used to make a getaway smooth?
Being used for the purpose of taking people
From place A to B
Kidnapping is illegal.
Traffickers don't care to ask for age, you see.
Continue to let your hate show
If that is the person you want to be
Me? I will take the advice given
just like it was meant
"As a warning and for awareness
Nothing more than that." Said she.

Talk

Whenever we talk
Your ears stop.
Ignoring all who oppose
Arguing and pitting
Friend to foe
Acknowledging only those facts that suit.
Moral code is a fine thing
ethics temper it.
Fear and hate are what you spread.
Choosing not to hear the sanity.
Common sense need not apply.
When facts are sourced by gossip,
woe to us, ostrich heads in the ground
accepting everything as is.
Dig deeper
Use the brain
They say, "it is never a good thing."
Too bad a left or a right I don't give.

Shan't

Shan't grin and bear it.
Nor smile and nod,
Keep laws off my body.
Fuck.
You.
All.

Word Of Advice

Did you not think this could happen?
Why?
Because it is just not done?
You are more fool than I, my dear.
I know it can happen
to me,
to anyone.
I may live under a rock.
Not knowing Who's Who
Nor caring about the next celebrity prop.
I do know.
What's out here
the evil and the good
though just because
it's expected that way,
"The bad only happens to the poor," you say.
That does not make it anymore right, any less
wrong.
It only happens to the other.
Not me, not you.
Not friend.
"Don't whine," says you.
You play act the victim.
It's not acting when it's true.
You are not me
You were not there
How do you know
The feelings,
The fear?
They are not weak
Not quite that young.
It could happen
Did to some.
You sit and judge
Calling out with hate and despise
When all I wanted to do was warn and advise.
You don't have to take it, nor agree
But maybe it saved someone

that is all it takes to validate me.
you can sit there and gripe
safe behind your screen
I will be there
when you say
Beware this almost...
did...
Tragically....
Happened to me.
I will not say mean words
or say it was your fault
I'm not one to rub other's wounds with salt.
Just remember as you sit there
In your bubbled sphere
There are many ways to end a world.
Most just need a pin, my dear.
When you need to rebuild yours.
I hope you find a friend.
And the next time you hear words of warning.
The response is thoughtful and wiser.
Not barbed to rend.

Don't Join the Feast

The oysters, they were tricked.
What is bad?
What do you know?
A sheep, like you?
What can you prove?
All you see
is what people
put into the world.
Is this the truth?
Is that all there is?
Did you check the facts?
The reality?
Take all at face value.
Did you think!
No, no.
The memes, the gifs
That is your news and the actual?
Has bias up the wazoo,
how can anyone make a real opinion?
Trying to digest information,
attacked by agendas
saying,
We need safe spaces,
Or is it compliant segregation
because our minds are being challenged
forced to see other points of view!
How dare!
How dare the world!
Not see, that the rock I live under
Is the reality of everything!
That what I see on my feed
is not real
because the internet
lies, not
The TV tells me all I need to know.
Backstabbing bastards bitch and moan
Lead the sheep to the fête.
Raise a glass,

To the walrus and the carpenter.
They will have
A wondrous feast.

Confusion

What is going on?
Where is my mind?
Why can't I say...do...
How did I get here?
When can I leave?
Is this how my life started?
Stopped?
How? What? Why?
I DON'T KNOW
I don't know
Uncertain
Always confused.
I can't even hear the call
Though maybe that is a choice.
Cowardice abounds, right?
Right?
RIGHT!?
All is confused torn asunder,
What the hell?
Heavens above.

I Matter

The things I need to say matter.
Trivial or not.
Every time we see each other,
I listen to you,
telling me the same thing once again.
I'm cut off.
Interrupted.
You stop me before I finish the first telling.
I need someone to listen to the prattle
inconsequential and insane.

Making time, it matters
shifting schedules, planning
Getting excited
Sitting and waiting
my questions ignored,
Via texts and calls.
Not showing
Soon, maybe?
Wait a little longer, you'll arrive.
Right?
Not letting me know
"Sorry. Something else came up."

I am a springboard
for all ideas.
When I try the same
crickets.
A shallow pool.
An empty bank.
Past deposits mean nothing.
I am stranded amidst my thoughts.
Nothing to bounce ideas off of.
To hear what I can't say
denying the undertow of my words
my writing.

I feel alone.

like no one understands.
'Cause when I make a request
none are listening
The advice?
Would have been different if you listened.
I want the same from you
as you expect from me.

I matter.
I need...
I just want...
...it's not
...a hard thing...
I need you to listen
hear me.
I matter.
And this?
It matters.
To me.

The Deafening Silence

When you're lost, alone
the deafening silence is daunting
a burden as you roam.
Searching the path
turning forward, circling back.
Wondering how your life tracks.
Obstacles form around you. A closing fist
creates pressure
choking, cloying, hard choices to make.

The deafening silence,
that heavy yoke.
Alone, surrounded by a room full of people,
all are talking, but for you it takes a toll,
connections you try and fail to make.
A deafening silence,
A silence that won't break.

Voiceless

I try to speak, my voice fails,
my pleads, cries of help
fall upon the rocks of closed ears
like ships wrecked on the shore
signs, lighthouses, ignored.
The people, the group are bought, sold
Making slaves of the sheep in the fold.
Sheep so dumb as to follow the Judas Goat.
Not thinking, not voting, not
challenging, nor changing
my voice soft-spoken falls on the empty void.
My Voice Screaming.
Ignored as feminine hysterics
Cast adrift forgotten, berated as Cassandra's tears.
Change be quick, or change be slow
Stagnation is death
rot
Moving row to row.

Shadow of a Bruise

Unlike the shadow of a bruise,
something that can be seen
if you know where to look,
The hollowness inside
deep and dark
pain is there
worse once it is pricked
an unhealing, gaping hole.
You want to cry!
Knowing it will not fill.
Try to find whatever will make it heal.
Be it lust or God,
a combination or more
We seek any fate, sense of fulfillment.
To feel hollow no more.

Such Sorrow

I cry in such sorrow
Knowing not what to do
The pain is real
Of what kind?
I have no clue.
I try to do what must be done
Still I'm doing nothing
maybe, try harder?
Push past, push through
The pain won
And I
cry inside all the harder
Where none can see this pain I feel
What is it doing to me?

Such sorrow
drowning inside
I try to shout
only silence comes out,
such sorrow I have.
It will not quit
pain without a scar
It won't go away.
The harder I try.
The deeper it goes
I don't want to wallow in my woes.
What do I do with such, such sorrow?
I just...
don't know.

Stuck Scream

Stuck,
in the throat
Chest tightening with the pressure
Building

Growing

No release
Though I try
Base of the clavicle
Up through the bronchi
Past the breastbone
To vibrate the larynx
Rip out my throat
Let loose the rage
Sorrow

Longing

A vessel that has known such sadness

Yet, full to the brim
Just tear it out
Let it rip through the throat
Scream

Let it all out
What is with the false starts?
Once out it will engulf the world
Unarticulated shouting
Let go
The loss
Sadness
Pain
Do others know my dolor?
Can they understand
If they heard it
Make them pause and wonder,
Shake their head,
Shiver like an earthquake.
Stay in the reality of their inner world
or seek out the pain?
Respond, knowing they're not alone?
How it builds
Builds
A hurting pressure
Waiting....
Waiting...
....Waiting... to go off...
Like a grenade
A landmine
Patient, ready to be tripped
If there is no release
Will I implode?
Will it be the once?
Causing hurt untold
To myself and others?

voiceless
In a world that won't ever
Shut-Up.
Speechless in a life that has a voice
the only ones to know of my passing
are family.
The song of the universe

has lost part of it's melody
never the same
A treasured being

Because there was no yell
no release
no explosion just implosion
I implore you
Please stuck scream
Please
Release.

Lost

Pusillanimous Soul

Foolish, foolish craven being.
Too coward to walk the daunting path.
There needs to be risk to be granted reward.
What greater reward than life?
Poor pusillanimous soul
Pity and contempt pointed your way,
advice given, ignored.
Yet still,
Too craven a being.
Stuck hard, stuck fast.
Becoming a rock upon a path
Feet planted, not from stubbornness,
but by fear of
failure? Insignificancy?
Things you have in spades,
mayhap, worse than needs be
The way daunting
To lift that
one
foot.
To try.
Pick it up
Left foot or right, it matters not
The attempt, the effort.
Life is not easy in any aspect.
But better a life than this
empty shell of a hollow existence
This state of nonbeing.
Poor Pusillanimous soul.
Too craven to try.
Too cowed to reach for the possible.

Monster

The monster is outside your head
All around it's under your bed
Tick
Tock
Knock
Knock

Stalking you forever more
Whose to know what's in store?
Tick
Tock
Rick
Rock

Pacing down the dreaming path
Creating a bloody bath
Tick
Drip
Nick
Rip

The monster roams through your mind
Ravaging all it can find
Drip
Drop
Chop
Flop

Leaving you a gaping wound
Bloodied thing of wrack and ruin
Tock
Tick
Drop
Drip

Road

I left the road,
Stepped off the path.
But where it went?
I do not know.
Trying to not get lost.
Wondering if I'd stumble upon a track.
What if I found another?
Hidden by branches.
hurdles disguised by vines,
would I walk away?
broken cobblestones, ancients stood here.
Do I walk in their wake,
or forge a new path.
I do not know.

Right now, though,
I am off the road.
How much shall I see?
I am so full of questions,
I might get lost.
How bad would that be?
Depends on what I would find.
Or lose.
Right now, I'm going somewhere.
I'll find out where, once I choose.

Where is the Good?

Look around.
The world has changed,
Sorrows shared,
Murdered life.
What has happened to the happy times?
All around you see destruction.
Hate is preached,
Love ignored,
How can you forget?
Love is strong.
But once flipped,
can hate be stronger?
No. No! That cannot be!
How can hate be stronger than love?
Does it mean it no longer exists,
Thoughts, memories, acts all told.
Because this bombardment of hate does not mean
love is less,
The dreams of the universe may be different,
They are still there.
Our choice
May be unclear
It might be gray.
Love is still a part of today.
Goodness and truth, though they may get in the way.
We see it every day.
The darkness, cannot win.
Evil won't seize the day.
As long as, we fight.
As long as we seek.
Every time we
Fight, struggle,
our best weapons:
Love, compassion, generosity
These things push back the despair
It may take many, it may take few.
So long as we are together.
Hand in hand

I know we will break through.
Past the hate
Beyond the greed
Our actions, our words
People will take heed.
One at a time or dozens on end
Those that are unclouded,
They are worth more than a hundred men.
It will be a struggle.
It is worth it,
Love always is.

Truth Not Lies

You think you know everything
When you truly know nothing
Everything that was your truth turns to lies
Fear not
There is always some truth in the world
God will never leave you
For he can see through the stars
He knows your deepest fears
He even cries your tears
You may not ever see Him,
If you look through human eyes
But never worry He always knows you
Even when you're in disguise
He is someone who will never let you down.
And catches you when you fall.
But don't forget the place He will never leave.
The place in your heart,
He won't leave it at all.

Fairytale

Pictures on the wall
Categorizing life
See the little children
What a loving wife.

Ribbons and trophies
Rewards throughout the years
Look how people come together,
Happiness outweighs the tears.

No picture-perfect houses
No dogs upon the stairs
A happier home you won't see though,
No monsters in their lairs.

Better than a fairy tale,
This home has no need for one.
A house full of laughter
A life well lived in adventure and fun.

Said

You said,
you said,
I could be anything I wanted.
Be anyone I needed.
I was told
That I could do anything I put my mind to
The only person stopping me,
was me.
Yet, out here in the world
I'm lazy.
I'm not enough.
"Don't be vain. Intellect is sexy,"
they tell me,
"Woman keep an empty brain."

You said,
You *said,*
All was possible,
Everything was within my grasp.
I just had to work for it.
The only thing to slow down my will,
was my drive.
Keep my nose to the grindstone,
Pull myself up by my
Bootstraps be broken.
and, in the real world, they say,
"Just be a good girl and smile,"
they pat my head,
"Stay barefoot in the kitchen, barefoot
in the bed."

I pursue my dreams,
every answer is "no."
I'm a tease, so rude.
Such, a know-it-all prude.
Designed to make wrong choices.
Too old to play pretend.
never young enough

Destined to fail in the end.

I didn't wait for you
I'm the boss calling the shots.
only to be a slut.
Wait a moment, I'm 'a frigid Bitch,' I thought.
That it? That's what you got?
I'll do as I please.
I shan't stop.
I'll flaunt it all,
Flaunt all I got.

Worry

Masked, you smile every morning,
in the afternoon, and evening too.
Remember you are loved.
(It is true.)

It's ok to cry when you're happy.
More so when you're sad.
Holding onto frustration and anger,
Scorches all amplifying the bad.

Worry is a bully
That worms its way in
Growing overwrought thoughts, baseless fears
Destroying peace of mind.
Leaving only a desolate shell when it wins.

If you are feeling helpless
squeezed between panic and despair,
sing a song and try to remember,
the good not the fear.

I hope these few words help you,
but if it's not your type of care,
I shall give you a hug.
Unless that is too much to bare.
I have this weighted blanket
to comfort, safe within its square.

Prison

A profile in shadow.
Could it be he?
Empty phrases charm.
Regifts of beautiful luxury,
fanciful images of picket fences
All with a sinister edge.

Look around with eyes unclouded.
In a prison of his whims.
Now you know,
he is no Romeo.
Try and save yourself,
yield not unto him.
Hie! Away from that place.
Never to return again.

It Is Said

In America
It is told
That all is equal.
Theory rarely meets practice.

In life
It is said
Every day is special
In truth we waste it.

In love
There is a saying
Love lost is better than none
Still, we flee from future pairing

In hope
It is believed
There is nothing so fragile
Trust broken by empty words.

Once

Once I sang till the sun rose.
Twice I danced with longing.
Thrice I cried 'til tears I had no more.
Fourfold I thought knew the score.

Once I failed to stand.
Twice I failed to give a damn.
Thrice bitterness over came.
Fourfold I knew I'd never be the same.

Foolish Mortals

Jump, Foolish Mortal.
Do as I command!
See the little ants,
walking in the sand.
They are content.
Have no fears.

Leap! Silly temporary ones!
I bid thee.
Watch the cows
chewing the cud.
What wonders they see!

Attend! Short lived beings.
Hear me for I have spoken!
Poor children lost in your
negative thoughts and ways.
Making the world harder,
putting hurtles in the path.

The universe.
It's not overly cruel!
Help each other.
This I did say.

The Day

Today is the day
You say
You're lonely.
Today is the day that you say
You care.
When we go out hand-in-hand with each other
Do people look and say, "there goes a nice pair?"

Today is the day
You say
You're so lonely.
Today is the day
That you say
You do care.
But when you're out and about with your boys
are you still lonely?
Cause I've been hearing stories from your friends.

Today is the day
You say
You're really so lonely.
Today is the day
That you say
You really do care.
But I've got to let you know
That you blew it.
Cause
Today is the day
That *I* say
I don't fuckin' care.

The Path

If only my pride
had not gone for the ride,
we'd've traveled like planned.
My temper hot,
wonderfully wroth.
in my pride
that I did abide,
heated departed we.
Though I did not know
Where the path doth go
I trod on sullenly.

After a year and a day,
I heard the way
Two friends fractured to foes.
I asked and listened,
To twits revisions
no two stories the same.
When the truth I found
I rent my pride
left myself raw and wide,
seeking forgiveness for my folly.
And you, my friend,
forgave in the end.
And together we resumed our journey.

Up in Arms

"To arms," says the boy.
To fight a righteous war.
"Up to guard," shouts the man.
He knows the corrupted truth.

"Time to fight," screams the lad.
Looking only at the glory.
"Death and blood," whispers the warrior.
Gory realities seen.

All go happy or sad
To fight and die for their country.
For honor and truth,
Stable work and pay,
Losing rights to save
With hope in a future.

"Into the battle," the young man yells.
Unknowing the death that awaits.
"Into the fray," the aged soldier agrees.
He knows the horrors ahead.

"Glory and honor," bellows the naive.
He doesn't understand.
"Destruction and torture," mummers the fighter.
Past nightmares terrorize.

All go in a line,
To die and fight for their country.
For the right and the brave,
For fear of the strange
Freedoms we seek.
All in hope of a future.

Protector

I wait upon the darkened shore.
A light to the hopeless
A guide to them, the huddled masses.
Haven for the forgotten, faceless.

My lamp held high, for all to see,
Yet, no one is allowed past me
A guiding protector I'd rather be
Then the guard they'd force,
By reforging shackles,
From whence—centuries ago—
I'd broken free.

Remembrance

The sun rises
Clouds flit across the sky
The day so normal and lazy
What happened was unexpected,
For the day started like every other
Seeming so calm, so peaceful
Nothing to mar it
Business as usual was the regard of most people

Dark clouds billowed past,
A tremor and shake
A wreck? An earthquake?
Was what we did think,
Yet, soon,
Too soon
Corrected were we.

A bomb in a van
Was all it took to shatter our safety.
Raced and went they
Quick and swift seeking our fallen.
Victims crying, many dying, both old and young.
As those far away helplessly watched as
the day wore on
"It could have been worse," very few said.
Our crisis teams were wonderful,
First responders, police and firemen.
A standard to be proud of and follow.

Some friends went home early,
And came back the next day.
Few came back a week later, still sad,
To our sympathetic dismay.
Hearts broken; worlds smashed.
Tornadoes left less devastation in their wake,
Then what happened because of that blast.

As the courts required,
We caught the men and trialed.
Justice the world did see.
Much changed as a result.
Not to mention remaking our lives and security.

And so, as it happens when catastrophe strikes
Something grew stronger,
The hope we called survivor,
Symbolized by a lone elm tree.
Resilient of spirit
The people of this state.
Refuse to lie down in surrender
From a tragedy caused by hate.

Year to year we run to remember,
Our lost, our people, how we came together,
Terrorists were not the victors in the
aftermath of that blast.
For we still live united and together.
Hoping that none would know our sorrow.
Unfortunately, that did happen,
A mere six years after.

Gate Keeper

Walking down the dirt path.
Darkness awaited me.
To my surprise, from a belt,
Death produced a key.
"I am the Gate Keeper," said he.
Opening a door into a garden,
Beautiful waterfalls, flowers everywhere.

I asked for Death's forgiveness,
To answer the mysterious knock
Forced to turn from eternity.

In my pajama pocket,
I found a secret token.
He was fine to wait a little while longer.
For Death bequeathed
My key to me.

Flight

Blunder about in the wilderness.
Go to the door.
Listen to the lore.
Knock four times to enter.
Go forth, go free,
Seek questions and answers.
Untethered over the moor.
Unbidden in your flight,
Glad to have listened
to the crone behind the door.

Seen

All I ask is to be seen.
That is it.
Yet, I know, even then,
I will not be happy.
God save me from fame.
I would be fine with well-known.
Isn't that what everyone wants?
To be seen?
To be known?
Somebody is terrifying.
Please don't let that happen to me.
A Nobody is what I want to be.
I still want you to see me,
Maybe that is what you want too,
What if I talked first?
Could we be friends?
I think I would,
see you.
Do you see me?
Could I be wrong?
You realize I can see you.
I smile,
And so do you.
All I want is to be seen.
I also want to be a nobody.
Can I be both?
Do you want that too?
Maybe we can
This should be simple,
plain and pure.
"Hello. How are you?"

The World I Need To Live In

Even though I never die,
My world continually ends.
People keep living,
oblivious.

Everything has changed,
and I build my world anew,
only for it to burst again.

The seasons turn
and things crumble.
I rebuild, refusing to give in.

I am a different person.
Then the one you did know.
No matter how much I look the same.

That is ok.
If you don't quite realize
Or understand,
I shall continually recreate and build once again.

Guide

The moon, guardian
Stars, guide.
The world a playground
Clouds a ride.

Do not dally, sally forth
From the prairie to mountain top.
Shout your name.
Off to obscurity
into the light.

Take a torch and seek,
all you hold dear.
Hold it past the end.

Fly
Small wings, they are,
shall grow as
you continue
Down the paths of the stars.

For The Shame

The shame of being.
 The despair of seemingly
Compared to each for existing as
A Bitch or Whore?

Shy blush of embarrassment
Face plain as day
Choosing one or two for the labeling of
Prude or crone for today?

The mask sparkles.
Brain full of fluff
Men chuckle and laugh saying:
"Hello pretty princess."
"Hello ditzy twit."
Condescending shit.

Too large for the average.
Skinny as a stick
Mockery and condemnation
Hundreds of words used
The wise know what to say and choose.

There may be no Queen, Beauty or Supreme
Without that evil undertone
For those who only like to skim
See nothing deeper, for the
shame upon them.

That's who to pity.
Not the witty
Those that stay at
the shallow end.

Moon

To the Moon, I love—
Let me
Show my love
through everything I say and do.

Cannot the moon turn the tide?
To have the power to make
The ocean bow down,
Thinking about it can be heady.
Turning even the best crazy.

Moon, without you, the sea
Would run free.
Thank you for being
safe, and don't corrupt
human spirits longing for power.
Stay out of reach,
now and forever.

People

People do,
what they say not to.
People say,
the opposite of what they do.
When you say you love me
Do you really?
You promise, swear it's true?

People hide and pretend
To be, who they are not.
Cheat others, then get offended when
it's done in return to them.
Do you lie? With your
body or soul? Can you be
honest and truthful?
Do you obfuscate that too?

Some say I'm crazy
Others say I'm wise.
I say, I'm silly
A child in disguise.
I trust you with my heart.
Bare my soul unto you.
My hope is you will save me
not
Throw me to the wolves.

Ransom

Ten pieces a ransom
Silver or gold
Either would be handsome
Too bad for you, him, I don't hold
Away from me, I'd gladly let him go
Force him to stay
I'd never be so low.

Ten pieces a ransom
Silver and gold
It matters not,
no sway, I hold.
'Tis *he* who wants
to be bought and sold.

Dream a Dream

Dreamer come to me
In spirit or in flesh.
Please come so I can see
Exactly what it is you dream.

To see a dream, lovely and true
Tis a gift from heaven.
Look within, Dreamer, please come through
So, I can dream a dream with you.

Fickle Love

Oh, do you love me?
Did you say you do?
Young love is so fickle.
Like the ocean blue.
Tell me that you love me.
Make sure I see it too.
Sometimes I get so lonely.
I hope you feel that too.
How is that other?
I know you love her more.
Kindness is not in staying.
I don't want to be with you, anymore.
Did you ever love me?
You said it was true,
So, now you say you love that woman.
Never felt like this before.
Fine. We are over.
Watch as I walk out the door.
Asking her: Do you love me?
Hearing her ask the same.
How like we were at the beginning.
Lust, not love, I saw today.
Now I see our folly.
I laugh as I walk away.
Love can be so fickle.
Caution is not love's way.

The Game

Upon the sky
You write a name,
Every day your changing the game.
Even though, somehow, I know
What's going on
Never have I seen your gaze
Eyes dark and cloudy
Crystal clear in the seams.
Such a fickle game.
Events unfolding, faster and faster
Ready? Do we need delay?
Yesterday was too late to tell you
Unfortunately, it can't be today.
Yes, tomorrow is a mystery.
Yet not that far to wait.
To tell you: I love you.
Unexpectedly, I control the game.

I was Lost

I was lost, likewise
found. The way of the world is askew.
Because of me or you?
Be it that we together, share
blame. Enough to go around.
What a shame. I will take
my part. Will you take yours?
Building is more fun together. Alone,
it is what it is.

I was lost. My name
Forgotten. No matter, no mind.
For I am Nobody.
Still,
Nobody slew a giant,
Nobody saved the world,
Nobody was a friend,
Maybe it is better than I had supposed.
I may not change the world
Outside my little sphere. Ripples tend to
Grow and spread no matter how slow
Until once more disaster strikes.
We'll rebuild again. To be lost or found
once more, my friend.

Peace

Release
A sigh,
Be at peace.
Breathe harm out of your body.
So that it may be recycled into good

Peace be in the
body,
Soul,
mind,
Contentment not contemptuousness
Need to contemplate

A world of peace.
How wondrous, how hard
Be at ease,
Not like a lion pacing in its cage
Like a cat sunning
By the garden window.

Light in the Darkness

Everything is asked for, the all and whole of it.
In return, nothing, not. a single. thing.
Step from the dark into the light.

Beware the fraud.
Forgo greedy, seedy lust.
Canopy blocking all,
pitching everything in darkness,
dancing shadows obscure the path.

Ask for the worthwhile one.
The one who gives as much as takes.
Receive the hand of love.
Share burdens.

Going forth in strength together.
Find the love that is yours alone,
Be the light in the darkness.

In the darkness be the light.

Always There

When I asked if you'd come
you told me in a while.
Then you told me to go ahead,
and that you soon, would follow.
I started to climb the stone
and after a little while
looked over the edge to find you
but I couldn't see you anywhere
I thought you didn't care.
And yelled, "Why aren't you there?"
After I resumed the climb
I started to cry.
And began to slip and fall
there you were to catch me
wipe away my tears
then you told me softly,
"Don't be scared nor frightened
I will always be there.
To hold you and comfort
I will always care.
And guide you down the trail.
I will always be there."
That was many years ago
but what you said was true.
You always comfort me
Always care.
You helped me in many ways,
In ways you might not ever know
The most important thing
about it was
Your word you kept, that you showed.

Sunshines

Wandering under the bright sunshine
Every day brings new surprises.
Blissfully happy traveling
Even when I lost my trail,
Lessons learned, passed along.
Regrets collected. Plans unfulfilled.
Clouds sometimes threaten, on occasion
Consume. If I can't pick myself up,
friends help me too.

Life's Dance

A dance
A dream
What fine things.

The world
So busy
Never to stop.

A meet-cute
A chance
I love you.

Life partners
Sacred vows
Happy family now.

Old age
Life fades
Death, restart.

Sly Smile

You looked at me with your
Sly, sly smile
With a small shimmy shake I said,
"Stay awhile."
A tête-à-tête,
Awhile yet,
Longing sighs,
Yours, not mine.
What next you said raised a blush
My reply was husky
Seductive and lusty
That sly smile grew a bit wild
By the time we were done
I left you
Breathless.

Our Hands

Give me your hand,
Reach as far as you can.
I will catch you,
Won't let you fall.
Give me your heart.
I shall treasure it.
Don't want to break it, I swear.

I'll give you my hand
Bring me close
Hold together
We'll weather any storm
To stay with you forever
In love, and whole
Alone nevermore
Nevermore.

Aurora

Skirting across the sky
Dancing steps only they know.
Free and joyous through the night
colors out to show
Dance across the bespeckled sky
They dance for themselves
Not you nor I
If lucky a patient sentinel be
The lights show themselves.
Watch what it looks like
To truly be free.

ToFrom

O

T

My, my

Stay

Let's go

F
r
o
m

Go

Stay
Go

Hi Bye

UP

Down

Skipping

We skip down the lane
silence not in our game.
Never we to stop our talking.
Dancing to music
only we can hear. Down the halls,
secrets galore. Taking notice of none.
Night descending too quickly, delight
escaping our parting.
Each day different from the last.
Daring us to more and more challenges,
useless is not in our vocab.
I had never been so happy,
having a friend like you.

Go Forth

Go forward
with confidence.
Do not tap dance as though on ice.
Plant your feet,
Take the steps now.
Boldly adventure.
On your journey,
move with daring,
see all there is to see.

The Journey

Does the way matter?
Does the path change?
Does the lesson lessen?
Does the way expand your understanding?
Answers you will get,
So long as the journey is taken.

Does it mean you've wasted your time?
Does being a nobody bother?
Does being somebody get in the way?
Does travel scare you?
There's a way to find out.
So long the journey is taken.

Forever and a day
Ending too soon
We shall see each other again.
So long, the journey, has taken.

The journey begins anew.

Acknowledgements:

There are many people who helped shape me as a person and a writer. I want to thank my grandma who encouraged me to grow and show my talents to the world. My nana who did write poetry on occasion, sadly she passed before my interest in poetry was spiked. I found Emily Dickenson shortly after Nana's death and those poems helped me process something I couldn't communicate. My English teachers who encouraged my poetry and writing in general, even my zoology class. (I wrote so I won't fall asleep in there.) I would also like to thank my school and local librarians thank you for not stifling my reading journey by letting me read things that I found interesting and pointed out authors and books. Thank you for listening to me. Sherry, thank you for the in-depth discussions we had. The amount of knowledge and faith you have is inspiring. I only hope to fill as large a faith cup as yours. I'm thankful to my parents who encouraged and helped me. You let me find my way and guided me when you could. You let my creativity and curiosity thrive, introducing me to different cultures, giving me an appreciation for different views. Writing groups also helped me in my writing journey. Shayla, Janie, Liz, Amanda, Natalie, and so many others helped give me the confidence to publish and continue to improve my writing. And thank you to my best friend Summer. You're an inspiration to me and one of the bravest people I know. Keep shining brightly. I'd like to thank my cover artist, Patty you're an amazing person thank you for helping me make my dream come true and taking my vague do this, try that, and creating these amazing covers. There are so many people to thank for support and help that I could write all day.

About the author

Cori June Thomas is from Yukon, Oklahoma. When she can she travels wherever the wind and her wallet takes her. Expanding her postcard collection when able and occasionally playing tourist in her own state. This is her first published work and is working toward publishing some fantasy and fiction novels.

You can find her on social media here:
Instagram: Cori_June_Author
TikTok: CoriJuneAuthor